Editors of Love
Patchwork & Quilting

LOVE Jelly Roll Quilts

A Baker's Dozen *of* Tasty Projects *for* All Skill Levels

Text, photography, and artwork copyright © 2020 by
Love Patchwork & Quilting (Immediate Media)

Publisher: Amy Marson

Creative Director: Gailen Runge

Acquisitions Editor / Editorial Compiler: Roxane Cerda

Managing Editor: Liz Aneloski

Cover/Book Designer: April Mostek

Production Coordinator: Zinnia Heinzmann

Production Editor: Jennifer Warren

Cover photography by *Love Patchwork & Quilting* (Immediate Media);
photography by *Love Patchwork & Quilting* (Immediate Media)

Published by Stash Books, an imprint of C&T Publishing, Inc., P.O. Box 1456,
Lafayette, CA 94549

Library of Congress Control Number:2019949096

Printed in the USA

10 9 8 7 6 5 4 3 2 1

contents

6

12

18

28

31

32

34

44

52

60

70

78

84

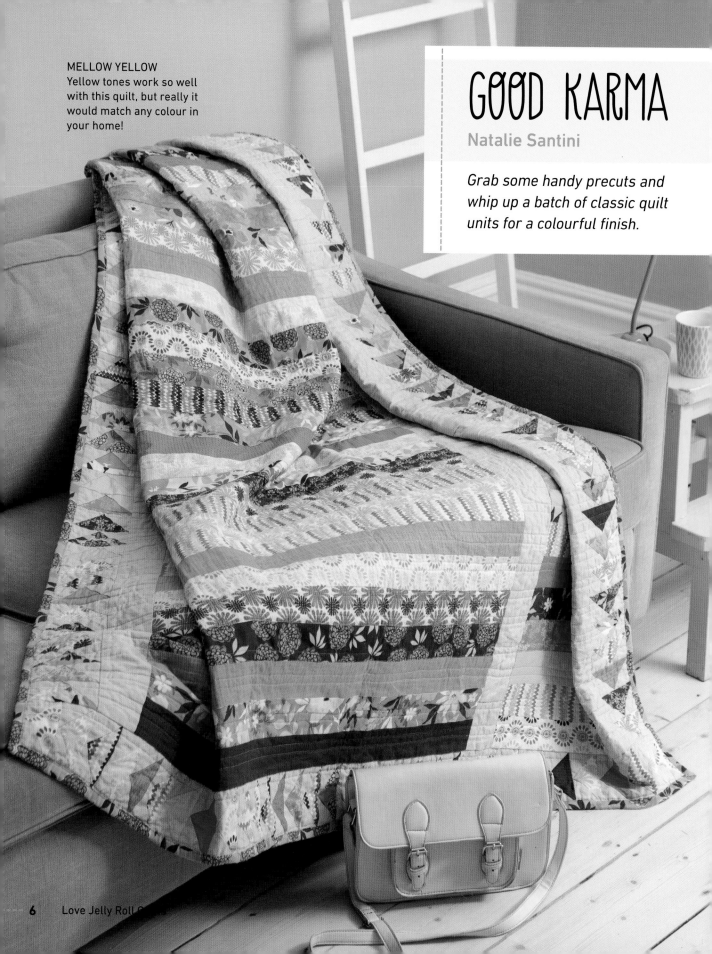

MELLOW YELLOW
Yellow tones work so well with this quilt, but really it would match any colour in your home!

GOOD KARMA

Natalie Santini

Grab some handy precuts and whip up a batch of classic quilt units for a colourful finish.

QUILT

Finished quilt:
56in × 71¾in approx

Fabrics used: Print fabrics are all from the Good Karma collection by Stephanie Ryan for Moda Fabrics + Supplies. Background fabric is Essex linen in Natural by Robert Kaufman Fabrics.

You Will Need

Print fabrics: Thirty-five (35) 4¾in squares and thirty-three (33) 2½in × WOF (42in) strips

Background fabric: 2yds

Backing and binding fabric: 4yds

Batting: 60in × 76in

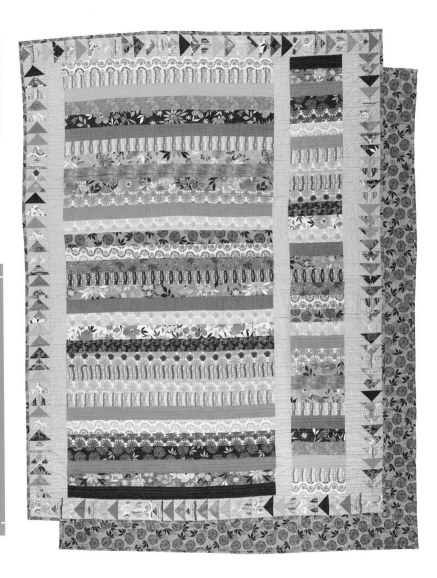

Note

You could use tonal solids instead of prints to create an eye-catching ombré effect.

Notes

- Seam allowances are ¼in, unless otherwise noted.
- Press seams open, unless otherwise instructed.
- RST = right sides together
- WOF = width of fabric
- Instead of cutting your own, you could use charm squares (trimmed to 4¾in square) and 2½in × WOF Jelly Roll strips.

Straight-line quilting complements the linear strip piecing.

Cutting Out ------------------------------------ ✂

1. From the background fabric cut three (3) 3½in × 65¼in strips (cutting parallel to the selvedge) for the sashing strips and one hundred and forty (140) 2⅝in squares for the Flying Geese.

2. From the backing and binding fabric cut seven 2½in × WOF strips for the binding. Set aside the remaining piece for the backing.

Making the Flying Geese

3. You will need one 4¾in print square and four 2⅝in background squares to yield four Flying Geese. Mark a diagonal line on the wrong side of all the background squares.

4. RST, place one background square on opposite corners of the print square, with the diagonal marked lines running from the outer corner to the centre of the print square. The squares will overlap where they meet in the centre. Stitch ¼in either side of the marked lines. *Fig. A*

5. Cut apart on the drawn lines and press open, making two Flying Geese. *Fig. B*

6. RST, place a background square on the remaining print corner of a unit made in Step 5, with the marked line running from the print corner. Stitch ¼in either side of the marked line. Repeat for the remaining background square and unit made in Step 5. *Fig. C*

7. Cut the units apart on the drawn line and press open, making four 4in × 2¼in Flying Geese. *Fig. D*

8. Repeat Steps 4–7 to make a total of one hundred and forty Flying Geese. You will need one hundred and thirty-eight.

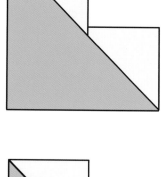

A

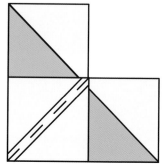

B

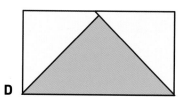

C

D

Piecing the Strip Sections

9. Take the 2½in × WOF print strips and lay them out, long edges together, to plan your design. Experiment with colour and print placement—you can piece from dark to light or in a random order. Join the strips to make a 66½in × WOF strip-pieced panel. To help prevent bowing, sew adjacent seams in opposite directions.

10. Trim the strip-pieced panel to 65¼in × WOF, trimming the panel evenly on both top and bottom.

11. Subcut the strip-pieced panel to give one 32½in × 65¼in rectangle and one 8½in × 65¼in rectangle.

Assembling the Quilt Top

12. Join a 3½in × 65¼in sashing strip to each long edge of the 32½in × 65¼in strip-pieced rectangle.

13. Rotate the 8½in × 65¼in strip-pieced rectangle by 180 degrees, so the fabrics are running in the opposite direction to those in the larger strip-pieced rectangle. Join the remaining sashing strip to the right-hand edge of this rectangle, then join the left-hand edge to the unit made in Step 12 to complete the quilt centre.

14. Take your Flying Geese units and lay them out, long edges together and all pointing in the same direction, into two strips of thirty-seven Flying Geese for the side borders and two strips of thirty-two Flying Geese for the top and bottom borders. Experiment with colour and print placement, as you did with the pieced strips.

15. Once you're happy with your layout, join the strips together to make two borders for the sides, each measuring 4in × 65¼in, and two borders for the top and bottom, each measuring 4in × 56½in.

16. Join the side border Flying Geese strips to each side of the quilt centre. In the left-hand border the units should all point upwards and in the right-hand border they should all point downwards—refer to the layout diagram for placement.

17. Join the top and bottom border Flying Geese strips to the quilt centre and side borders. In the top border the units should all point left and in the bottom border they should all point right.

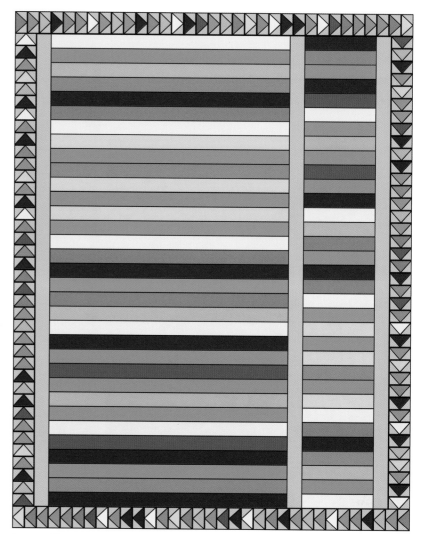

Layout diagram

Quilting and Finishing

18. Take the backing fabric set aside in Step 2 and cut it in half across the WOF. Then remove the selvedges and re-join the pieces along the length. The backing needs to be least 2in bigger all around than the quilt top.

19. Make a quilt sandwich by placing the backing fabric right side down, the batting on top, then the quilt top centrally and right side up. Baste the layers together.

20. Quilt as desired. Natalie quilted pairs of lines ½in apart at 1in intervals. Trim any excess batting and backing.

21. Sew the binding strips together end to end using diagonal seams. Press the seams open and trim away the dog-ears. Fold in half lengthwise, WST, and press.

22. Sew the binding to the right side of the quilt, folding a mitre at each corner. Before completing your stitching, neaten the short raw end of the starting piece and insert the ending piece into it.

23. Fold the binding over to the back of the quilt and finish by hand stitching in place.

GRANNY SQUARES

Jo Avery

We're channelling the vintage crocheted granny blanket look with this super quick and easy quilt-as-you-go project.

Make it in a day!

RETRO GEOMETRICS
Don't let crocheters have all the fun—you can sew and quilt a classic granny square, too! The concentric squares are easy to piece using nostalgic prints for a retro chic style.

QUILT

Finished quilt:
59in square approx

You Will Need

Central fabric: 3½in square

Print fabric: 2½in strips,
3yds in total

Batting: 63in square

Backing fabric: 3½yds

Binding fabric: ½yd

Basting spray (*optional*)

Note

This project is a great scrap buster
and especially good for leftover
Jelly Roll fabric strips.

Tip

Try using strips in gradually
lighter shades of the same
colour for a modern ombré
colour scheme.

The geometric squares are utterly mesmerising.

Cutting Out

1. From the binding fabric cut six (6) 2½in × WOF strips.

Piecing the Quilt

2. Prepare the backing fabric by cutting the yardage into two equal
lengths. Remove the selvedges and sew together along the length
with a ½in seam allowance. Press well and trim to 63in square.

3. Lay the batting onto a flat surface and place your backing, right
side up, on top. Peel back half of the backing and spray layers with
basting spray. Carefully lay the backing fabric back over the batting,
smoothing out any wrinkles. Repeat with the other side. Alternately,
you can secure your batting with safety pins but these will need to
sit on the batting side so you can easily remove them as you work.

Each fabric strip is quilted in place as you sew.

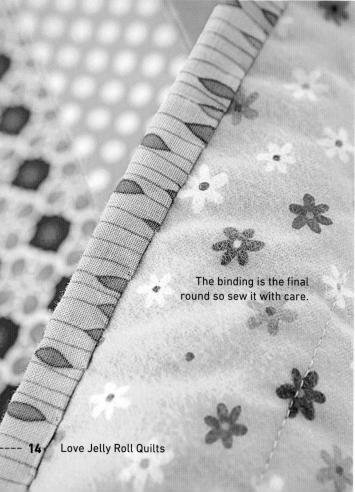

The binding is the final round so sew it with care.

4. Fold your backing/batting in half, towards the backing, then fold in half again so that you can see a centre cross on your batting side. Mark this with a pencil or removable pen.

5. Fold your 3½in square in half and in half again, right sides together, and line this up with the centre cross on your batting. Pin the square in place, right side up.

Tips for Strip Piecing

After sewing a fabric strip, trim it as accurately as you can.

Use the middle of the block to line up your next strip, not the end of the strip you have just attached because this will not have been as accurately cut as your strip sides.

Make sure you really open out your seams when you finger-press them. Give your work a proper press after every few rounds.

6. Take your first 2½in strip and place right sides together with one side of the square, lining up the edges exactly. Pin then sew in place. *Fig. A*

Trim the strip in line with the centre square and finger-press the seam open. *Fig. B*

7. Lay your next strip along the next edge of your square, moving clockwise and including the edge of the last strip. *Fig. C*

Pin, sew and trim to line up. Continue placing strips around your square in this fashion until the centre square is surrounded. *Fig. D*

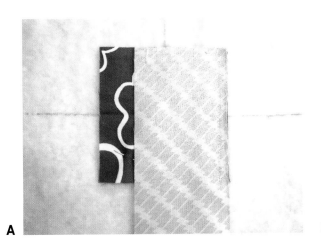

A

B

C

D

8. Begin your next "round" using a different coloured strip and start at a different corner of the square (this well help prevent distortion as your quilt grows). Pin and sew strips, trimming to size as you go. Roll the excess batting/backing so that it fits in your machine throat. *Fig. E*

We made each round a different colour, sewing together smaller strips where longer pieces were needed and mixing prints of the same colour within a round. *Figs. F & G*

9. Keep going until you have completed fourteen rounds. Trim your batting and backing to square up. *Fig. H*

Piecing the Quilt

10. Prepare the binding by sewing the six strips end to end to form one long length. Fold along the full length, wrong sides together and press. Use this to bind the quilt.

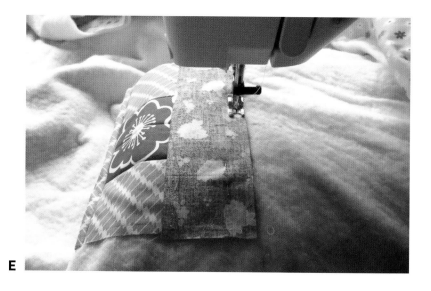

E

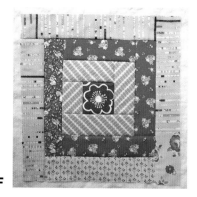

F

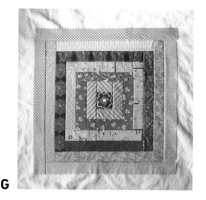

G

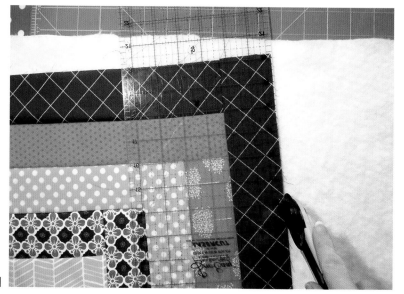

H

Switch up your colour palette with each round. Jo's rainbow hues are gorgeous, but we think this would look fab in two-tone stripes!

DRYSLWYN DREAMS

Susan Briscoe

This reinterpretation of an Edwardian Welsh scrap coverlet is an ideal project for Jelly Roll strips or charm squares. The original coverlet had no batting but was quilted in waves (zigzags) and circles. This modern version is simply quilted in the ditch between rounds.

The vibrant blue-and-white polka dot fabric makes a striking accent colour next to the rich, autumnal browns and reds.

QUILT

Finished quilt:
60in square approx

You Will Need

Forty-one (41) Jelly Roll strips* for the "scrap" fabrics *or* **one Jelly Roll and five 5in charm squares**

Polka dot fabric (blue): 1yd

Backing fabric: 64in square minimum (This can be pieced.)

Batting: 64in square (The sample quilt used 80/20 cotton/poly batting.)

Machine sewing thread to tone with fabrics

Hand or machine quilting thread to tone with fabrics

* Forty-one (41) Jelly Roll strips is the absolute minimum you can use for this quilt. It doesn't allow for cutting errors and gives little choice about fabric placement, so it's best to have a few extra 2½in strips, charm squares or other scraps to mix in. There are usually forty strips in a Jelly Roll. You can cut four 4¼in strips and six 4in strips from one 42in Jelly Roll strip (or two 4¼in strips and eight 4in strips) with very little wastage. With a standard forty-strip Jelly Roll you would be short of just ten pieces, which could be cut from charm squares or other scraps.

Symmetry in Quilts and Blocks

The Dryslwyn quilt is a beautiful example of symmetry. Where a layout is symmetrical across vertical, horizontal and diagonal axes, *directional symmetry* is at play. *Reflective symmetry* shows the pattern duplicated across only one axis (as if using a single mirror to create the effect). Visual movement can be created using *rotational symmetry*, where a pattern is repeated over 360 degrees in a series of equal turns. A common example is every 90 degrees, perfect for the shape of most quilt blocks and quilts.

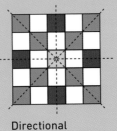

Directional

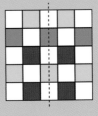

Reflective

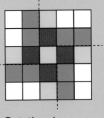

Rotational

Behind the Quilt

Dryslwyn Coverlet

Susan's inspiration for this quilt was a photo of a scrap patchwork coverlet (a coverlet has no batting inside) from Dryslwyn, from Jen Jones' collection in Janet Rae's book, *Quilts of the British Isles*. It is a combination of leftover strips from two Jelly Rolls that had been cherry picked for another project, along with some charm squares. "The quilt is constructed in rounds from the centre outwards, like a medallion quilt or a giant Log Cabin block, and working out the strip sizes was a little tricky," explains Susan, "with two slightly different strip lengths needed to make the borders fit." The original maker played with subtle reflective and rotational symmetry in the patch arrangement, repeating the fabrics and alternating between light and dark prints in the consecutive borders to give the patchwork a very appealing rhythm. The many colourways of each print pattern suggest it was made from fabric samples, including florals, geometric prints and stripes. The patches in the original coverlet were wider than 2½in Jelly Roll strips, so while this quilt is just 60in square (rather than the original's 73in × 68in), it has more rounds (borders) than the original (which also had two additional patchwork strips at the top and bottom to make it rectangular). Make the quilt larger or smaller simply by adding or removing borders, following the stepped strip sequence. The quilt is finished with a traditional knife-edge, where the front and back are folded in together and slipstitched around the edge, but you can bind it if you prefer.

Choosing Fabrics and Colours

1. This relatively simple patchwork design relies on fabric placement for interest. Susan based her fabric colour placement on the original for the first ten rounds, but you can play around with this arrangement to suit fabrics of your choice. Susan also included lots of paisley prints, as paisleys were so popular with Welsh quilters. Divide the strips into light and dark prints, with about six more strips allocated to the dark selection than the light. You will have some darker lights and some lighter darks, but that is fine. It is best not to cut all the strips at once or you could be a little overwhelmed with piles of fabric. Cut them as you go, a round at a time, and take time to arrange the prints. You can use a smaller cutting mat for this, if you have one. Follow the photo of the quilt and the two piecing diagrams (pages 24 and 25) to check the placement of accent prints like the reds and yellows. Of course you can make up your own arrangement of fabrics if you prefer, remembering to alternate between light and dark prints in every other round. You will usually need two or four pieces of each fabric to maintain the symmetrical rhythm. Take care when selecting the fabrics for the first few rounds, as this will be the focal point of your quilt and you may have fabrics you would like to feature here. If you need to use up small pieces and have only one of some A or B patches, save these for the outer rounds.

Cutting Out

2. From the Jelly Roll strips (and additional fabrics you may be using) cut the following.

- Four (4) 4½in × 2½in strips (for round 1 of the quilt centre).

- One hundred and four (104) 4¼in × 2½in strips (the A pieces—twenty-six (26) per side of the quilt).

- Three hundred (300) 4in × 2½in strips (the B pieces—seventy-five (75) per side of the quilt).

3. From the polka dot fabric cut the following.

- One (1) 4½in square for the quilt centre.

- Fifty-six (56) 2½in squares (cut from three and a half 2½in × WOF strips).

- Three hundred and sixty-four (364) 1in × 2½in strips (cut from nine 2½in × WOF strips).

Making the Patchwork

4. Start by making the quilt centre. Follow the exploded assembly diagram (page 25) and with a ¼in seam allowance, assemble the quilt centre like a Nine-Patch block, using the 4½in square, four (4) 4½in × 2½in strips and four (4) 2½in squares. There are two (2) pinkish red and two (2) pink 4½in strips on opposite sides of the centre square—think of these as round 1. Press each seam to one side, alternating the pressed seam direction so the pieces butt against each other and the seam allowances line up.

5. Now piece the quilt in rounds (as shown by the numbers in the exploded assembly diagram, page 25). Each subsequent round is made up of four (4) long pieced strips. Each pieced strip has an A piece at each end and, apart from round 2 (which is two A pieces only), the other pieces in every strip are B pieces. These pieces are joined by the 1in × 2½in polka dot strips and the seam allowances are pressed towards the narrower strips each time. Join one 1in × 2½in piece to each A or B piece as relevant and then join these units together in pairs to make each strip, joining pairs to make fours and so on (rather than adding pieces to just one end of an ever-increasing and unwieldy long strip). The patchwork strips at the top and bottom of the

quilt have 2½in squares at the ends. The seam is pressed away from these squares, *towards* the A pieces. Sew the patchwork strips *without* the corner squares to your patchwork first and press the seam allowance towards the outside of the patchwork. Then sew the strips with the corner squares to the main patchwork piece and press outwards again. On each round, assemble the patchwork strips as you go, selecting and placing your fabrics with care. Use the photos and diagrams as a guide (or make up your own arrangement), playing with reflective and rotational symmetry. (See the diagrams in Symmetry in Quilts and Blocks, page 19.)

6. Round 2: Dark

This is a good place to feature striking prints. The eight (8) larger pieces are all A pieces. If your fabrics are directional, arrange them so the pattern is moving away from the quilt centre. Think about symmetry if using large motifs—this round uses rotational symmetry to alternate between two similar paisley motifs, from red and blue colourways of the same pattern. Rotational symmetry means the fabrics will progress in sequence around the patchwork rounds or borders. The original coverlet has the same print in different colourways in this round.

7. Round 3: Light

This is the first round with B pieces, which accent the patchwork strip with yellow ochre prints on each side. The original patchwork has yellow on the sides but cream at the top and bottom. The A pieces in Susan's quilt are four different colourways of the same print, arranged with rotational symmetry.

8. Round 4: Dark

The fabric patterns are arranged with reflective symmetry (a mirror image) but the colours of the prints are arranged to have rotational symmetry,

so a red colourway is directly opposite a blue but diagonally opposite the same print. The original quilt has just four patterns in different colourways in this round.

9. Round 5: Light

In this round, the central B piece in each strip is the same pinkish red or pink print used in the quilt centre. The other pieces follow rotational symmetry, with each patchwork strip having a yellow print and a cream print at either end. The prints on either side of the pinkish red are the same, but are different from the prints on either side of the pink print—only the background colours are the same. The original has the same design for the A pieces but their arrangement is not perfectly symmetrical, as it looks like the maker didn't have enough of pieces with more yellowish backgrounds and the patch at the top of the right-hand side has a white background.

10. Round 6: Dark

The A pieces are arranged as a mirror image of each other, as in the original, with the same prints on both ends of the side patchwork strips and the top and bottom strips, but the B pieces follow rotational symmetry. The two central B pieces on each side are striped prints, similar to those used on the original patchwork.

11. Round 7: Light

All pieces here are arranged with rotational symmetry. The A pieces have the same light blue background but are two different prints. The central B patches are two different directional fabrics, with the same fabric opposite itself. Four yellow B patches are included in this round. The original coverlet seems more randomly pieced at this stage, with the maker having enough of some fabrics to place them symmetrically, while others use substitutes of similar value, colour or pattern.

12. Round 8: Dark

Most of the pieces in this round are arranged with rotational symmetry, apart from the A pieces, which are the same print on every corner but in two different colourways, with the same colourway on either side of the corner square. In the original, the A pieces are mirror images of each other, with the same print in two slightly different colourways, so the A pieces are the same top and bottom, and on both sides. There are two striped B pieces in the centre of each strip, as per the original. Note the position of the red pieces.

13. Round 9: Light

As you move away from the centre perfect symmetry becomes less important in the original coverlet's layout, but fabrics are still matched in the more obvious places, like the strip centres or either side of the corner squares. The new patchwork arrangement is mainly reflective symmetry, with A patches and the central B patches mirroring each other, top to bottom and side to side (red prints on the sides). The B patches either side of the centre patch are all the same print and colourway. The remainder of the B patches, including two colourways of the same stripe, are mirrored diagonally, top to bottom and side to side.

In keeping with the original tradition, Susan has backed her quilt with a paisley print popular with Welsh quilters of the time.

14. Round 10: Dark

The original coverlet has only ten rounds and the final round is relatively random, with the centre B pieces matching each other on that strip only while there are more similar (but not identical) mirrored matches between the A pieces. Two extra strips, added to both the top and the bottom of the rectangular original coverlet, are also quite random, although more striking prints have been carefully placed. Susan's patchwork has mostly reflective symmetry in this round, with the A pieces mirroring each other in the same fabric but different colourways and the adjacent B patches all in the same striped print. Note the red prints. The two brown print B pieces in the centre of each strip are arranged rotationally, with the same fabric on either side of these pairs.

15. Round 11: Light

All the pieces are arranged with complete reflective symmetry, so they mirror each other horizontally and vertically across the quilt. There is a central red B piece top and bottom.

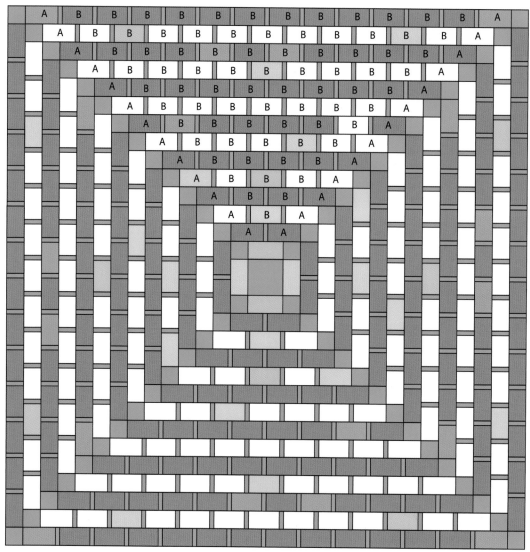

Layout diagram

16. Round 12: Dark

The A and the first three B pieces at each end of each strip mirror each other, with two different fabrics for the A pieces and the same selection for the B patches. The remaining four patches in the centre of each side have rotational symmetry. Note the reds and the stripes.

17. Round 13: Light

This round is a mixture of reflective and rotational symmetry, starting to use up the remaining fabrics. The striped A pieces mirror each other across the patchwork in two slightly different colourways. The light blue B pieces mirror each other, with two

prints with the same background colour, one used top to bottom and the other side to side. Note the reds and the stripes. At this stage, arrange whatever fabrics you have left in a way that pleases you.

18. Round 14: Dark

In this final round the blue B patches mirror each other, but all the other pieces have rotational symmetry, with one set of fabrics for the side strips and another for top and bottom. There is repetition of the same print in different colourways, including the A pieces, two identical prints in brown and red colourways.

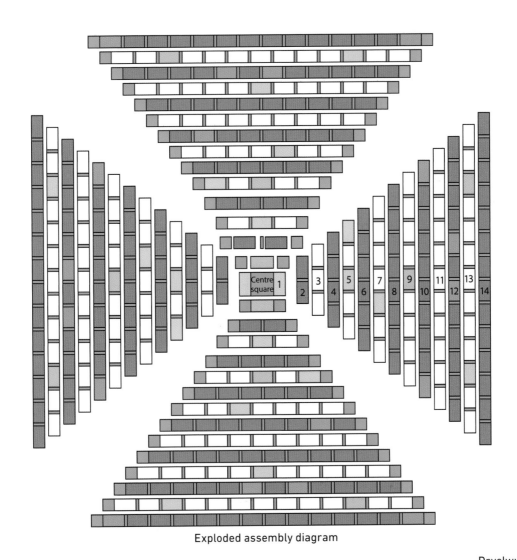

Exploded assembly diagram

Quilting

19. Layer the backing, batting and quilt top and tack (baste), using your favourite method. Hand or machine quilt in the ditch along each strip. Zigzags could be added to reflect the original coverlet's quilting in waves, or circular motifs incorporated into the quilting pattern. The quilting on old Welsh quilts rarely follows elements in the patchwork design, so even all-over longarm pantograph patterns could be appropriate if you want a machine-quilted piece.

Creating the Knife-Edge Finish

20. Old British coverlets and quilts usually have a knife-edge finish rather than a binding, unlike most modern quilts. Of course, you could use a standard double-fold binding if you wish. To make a knife-edge, trim the backing and batting to the same size as the patchwork. Hand or machine quilt all around the quilt, 1in from the edge. Separate the edges of the patchwork top and backing fabric and trim ¼in off the edge of the batting all round with scissors, taking care not to clip the backing or patchwork as you do so. If it helps, pin the patchwork and the backing fabric folded away from the edge. Don't worry if the edge of the batting is slightly wavy, as tiny amounts of excess batting will be hidden in the edge finish.

21. Turn in a ¼in seam allowance all round the quilt. Turn in the backing first, overlapping the batting. Place the pins at right angles to the quilt edge, pointing towards the quilt centre, so you can pull the pins out later. Fold under a ¼in hem all round the patchwork and pin, lining up with the edge of the backing and keeping the edge as straight as possible. Slipstitch or ladder stitch the edge of the patchwork to the edge of the backing. At each corner, fold in the seam allowances of the back and front of the coverlet square but in opposite directions and overlap them before tucking them in, as shown. *Fig. A*

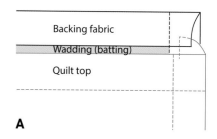

Backing fabric

Wadding (batting)

Quilt top

A

22. This step is optional: You could quilt another line all around the coverlet a ¼in from the edge or midway between the edge and the previous quilting line. Many traditional British quilts have a second line or third line of quilting, which gives a firmer, flatter edge. Don't forget to add a label to help people identify your work in the future.

Tip

Take care to line up and pin each strip in place before sewing, pinning at right angles to the seam and removing the pins as you sew. The narrow blue polka dot strips need to line up on alternate rows and, unless you pin, they will shift out of alignment as you sew. While there are no seam allowances to match up from one round to the next, the pattern made by the narrow strips would be lost if the strips are allowed to shift while you sew.

To achieve a truly traditional look for your quilt, use the knife-edge finish instead of binding the edges. See Creating the Knife-Edge Finish (previous page) for more details.

Love that fleece fabric!

CUDDLE UP

Alice Hadley

This little trio of makes comes together in an afternoon, perfect for last-minute gifting!

ALL ABOUT POSY
This little set all started with a Jelly Roll of Posy by Aneela Hoey. It's full of pretty prints and fresh colours that are just right for brightening up a baby's room.

QUILT

Finished quilt:
30in × 42in approx

You Will Need

Linen fabric: 1yd

Assorted print fabrics:
One hundred and sixty (160)
2½in squares

Binding fabric: ⅜yd

Batting: 34in × 46in

Backing fabric: 34in × 46in

Embroidery thread for
quilting

Notes

• Seams are ¼in throughout, unless otherwise stated.

• We used a Jelly Roll to cut all of the print fabric squares and bind the quilt (with several lengths of fabric left over!).

• Finish the raw edges of the linen fabric with a zigzag stitch to prevent fraying.

Tip
When you're mixing different fabrics (linen, cotton and fleece), it's really important to prewash!

When the piecing is simple, you can spend more time on fabric and finishing touches!

Cutting Out

1. From the linen cut eleven (11) 2½in × 30½in pieces.

2. From the binding fabric cut four (4) 2½in × WOF strips.

Piecing the Rows

3. Arrange your fabric squares in ten rows, with sixteen squares in each. If your fabrics feature directional prints, take care to position them all the correct way up. Sew the squares together in pairs, then

sew the pairs together, repeating until you have pieced each row. *Fig. A*

Trim 1in from each end block—each row should measure 2½in × 30½in. *Fig. B*

4. Lay out your quilt top, placing a linen strip at the top and bottom of the quilt, and alternating a print row with a linen row, as shown. Sew the rows together. *Fig. C*

Finishing the Quilt

5. Place your quilt top on your batting and baste in place. Quilt as desired. We used three stands of embroidery floss to stitch an *X* in the corner of each pieced row, tying at the back of the wadding to secure. Remove your basting stitches or pins. *Fig. D*

6. Place your quilt on top of your backing fabric, wrong sides together. Baste using your preferred method—we pinned and then ran a line of basting stitches around the outer edges of the quilt (these stitches were hidden by the binding). Square up the quilt top and trim away excess batting and backing fabric.

7. Join the binding strips end-to-end to make one long length. Use to bind the quilt, taking care the mitre the corners. We used four different Jelly Roll strips to give our quilt a fun patterned binding.

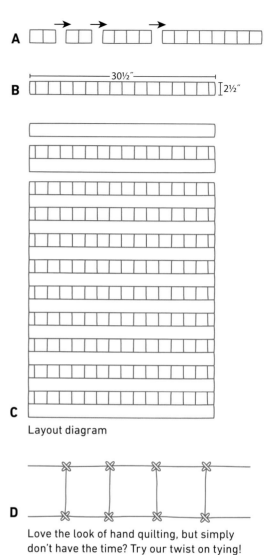

Layout diagram

Love the look of hand quilting, but simply don't have the time? Try our twist on tying!

Quilt Labels

A label is the perfect way to personalise a special gift, or mark a special occasion. Make sure to include the name of the recipient as well as your own name.

To make a label like ours, add your embroidery to a large square of linen. Give your label a good press on the reverse. Centering your stitching, trim the label into a rectangle, leaving a ¼in seam allowance on all four sides. Layer over a piece of batting, cut to the same size and bind the edges as you would a quilt. Add the label to your quilt using invisible stitches.

CUSHION

Finished cushion:
16in square approx

You Will Need

Linen fabric: 16½in square

Assorted print fabrics:
Eight (8) 2½in squares

Batting: 17in square

Fleece backing fabric:
16½in square

Embroidery thread for quilting

Polyester stuffing

Add a little lilac in place of pink for a fresh look.

Note

We used the leftover Jelly Roll fabric from the quilt (page 29) to make both the cushion and the comforter.

Cutting Out

1. Cut the linen into two pieces:

- 6in × 16½in
- 9in × 16½in

Piecing the Rows

2. Arrange the print fabric into a row of eight and sew together, pressing the seams to one side. Trim to 2½in × 16½in.

3. Sew the pieces of linen to the top and bottom of the strip, and trim to 16½in square.

4. Place your cushion top on your batting and baste in place. Quilt as desired. We used a couple of rows of running stitch, either side of the patchwork panel. Trim away any excess batting.

5. Place the cushion front and cushion back right sides together and pin in place. Mark the curved corners with a removable fabric pen and then sew around all four sides, leaving a 4in turning gap in the bottom.

6. Turn right sides out, stuff, and stitch the turning gap closed by hand.

Finishing Touches

If you want to create an envelope closure for the back of your cushion, you will need to add some fusible stabiliser to the back of your fleece fabric to give it structure.

COMFORTER

Finished comforter:
16½in square approx

You Will Need

Linen fabric: 17in square

Assorted print fabrics:
Nine (9) 2½in squares and
eight (8) 2½in × 5½in strips

Backing fabric: 17in square

Batting: 17in square

Embroidery thread for
quilting

Note

We used the leftover Jelly Roll
fabric from the quilt (page 29) to
make both the cushion and the
comforter.

Babies love to play with different textures—but remember,
everything *will* end up covered in dribble!

Cutting Out

1. Cut the linen into two pieces:

• 6in × 17in

• 11in × 17in

Piecing the Comforter Top

2. Arrange the print fabrics into a row of nine and sew together,
pressing the seams to one side. Trim approximately ¾in from each
end for a row measuring 2½in × 17in.

3. Sew the pieces of linen to the top and bottom of the strip, and trim
to 17in square.

4. Place your cushion top on your batting and baste in place. Quilt as
desired. We used a couple of rows of running stitch, either side of the
patchwork panel.

Prepare the Tabs

5. Take one of the 2½in × 5½in strips and press in half, wrong sides together, along the length. Now fold the long raw fabric edges into the central fold and press. Repeat for all eight (8) fabric strips. *Fig. A*

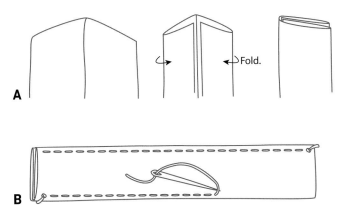

A

Fold.

6. Using three strands of embroidery thread, sew a running stitch up and down the two long edges of each of the tabs. *Fig. B*

Alternatively, you could topstitch on your sewing machine.

B

Assemble the Comforter

7. Position the tabs along the bottom edge of the comforter front—align the raw fabric edges of the tabs with the edge of the comforter, with the fold pointing into the centre of the comforter top. Pin in place.

8. Place the backing fabric right sides together with the comforter front, sandwiching the tabs between the two layers. Pin in place.

9. Mark the curved corners with a removable fabric pen and then sew around all four sides, leaving a 4in turning gap in the top (opposite the tabbed edge).

10. Turn right sides out, press and then stitch the turning gap closed by hand.

SUPER STRIPS MEDALLION QUILT

Susan Briscoe

Jelly Rolls really come into their own when lots of long strips are required, but this medallion quilt can also be made from strips cut from fat quarters, as the longest 2½in-wide strip only needs to be 18½in for the pieced sections, with additional yardage for the frames. Because the strips are sewn into squares and rectangles before cutting out the large triangles, it is quick and easy to make.

Bright retro fabrics in a heritage inspired design— what's not to love about this fabulous quilt?

QUILT

Finished quilt:
61in square approx

You Will Need

One Jelly Roll *or* an assortment of fat quarters* cut into strips along the width of fabric

Fabric for frames: 1 m or ¾ m if including a fabric from the Jelly Roll

Binding fabric: ½yd

Backing fabric: 65in square minimum (This can be pieced. Susan used a plain cream calico.)

Batting: 65in square (The sample quilt used Hobbs Polydown.)

Machine sewing thread to tone with fabrics

Hand or machine quilting thread to tone with fabrics

* Susan suggests using a minimum of twenty (20) fabrics to give enough variety, preferably a few more. Fewer fabrics mean more repetition in the patchwork. You won't use all of the fat quarter to cut the strips, so there will be plenty of fabric left over for another project. You could use them for a coordinating pieced backing.

Alternatively, if you want a larger version of the quilt, you could use the remnants to add extra triangle strip sections or borders.

Fabric used: Katie Jump Rope by Denyse Schmidt for FreeSpirit Fabrics

Notes

- Use ¼in seams and a short stitch length (1.8 mm or less) throughout.
- Pin strips together before sewing, with pins at right angles to the seam.
- Follow the pressing instructions for each frame.

Behind the Quilt

Super Strips Medallion Quilt

The zingy strip design is based very loosely on *The Hearts and Crosses Coverlet*, a nineteenth-century strip-pieced patchwork in the Quilters' Guild of the British Isles' collection, which is made from narrower strips. We sorted our retro-style fabrics into warm and cool colours for the centre contrast and shaded the outer borders from warm to cool, and added frames in a red miniprint from the same range. Alternatively, you could try a light-to-dark variation. Susan has taught Super Strips as a workshop quilt for a number of years and there are many student variations illustrated on her blog. To see dozens of variations, visit susanbriscoe.blogspot.co.uk > Labels > Super Strips Quilt Top.

Technical Tip

Sewing multiple strips together often results in a cumulative width discrepancy if your seam allowances are not perfectly ¼in. The strip-pieced centre may be slightly smaller than anticipated. Rather than waste time unpicking, from Step 4 onwards, measure the quilt top through the centre before cutting and sewing the next frame or border and simply adjust frame or border sizes to fit.

Cutting Out

1. From the Jelly Roll cut as follows:

- Nine (9) warm (or dark) 18½in long strips.

- Nine (9) cool (or light) 18½in long strips.

- Thirty-four (34) 15¼in long strips for the outer triangles—one from each of the remaining Jelly Roll strips, and the rest from twelve (12) of the leftover lengths of warm and cool strips above.

- Eighty-eight (88) 7in strips

- Ten (10) warm 7in strips for the faux mitred border sections.

- Ten (10) cool 7in strips for the faux mitred border sections.

2. From the frame fabric cut as follows:

- Thirteen (13) 2½in strips across the WOF (eleven or twelve strips will do if you are using some fabric from your Jelly Roll). Sew together five (5) of your strips into one length and subcut as follows:

Two (2) 24⅞in × 2½in strips for the inner frame.

Two (2) 28⅞in × 2½in strips for the inner frame.

Two (2) 40½in × 2½in strips for the middle frame.

- Sew together the remaining eight (8) strips then subcut as follows:

Two (2) 44½in × 2½in strips for the middle frame.

Two (2) 57½in × 2½in strips for the outer frame.

Two (2) 61½in × 2½in strips for the outer frame.

Making the Centre Diamond

3. If you are using some of the Jelly Roll strips for the frames, remove the one or two strips that match the frame fabric and put these to one side. Arrange the nine (9) 18½in warm strips in a sequence that pleases you and do the same for the nine (9) cool strips. With right sides together and pinning along the strip so the ends match up, sew the strips together in pairs along the long side. Sew pairs together into groups of four (4) and continue until all nine (9) strips of each group are sewn together, to make an 18½in square. Repeat with the cool strips. Press the seams on the cool square towards the centre strip and the seams on warm square from the centre strip outwards. *Fig. A*

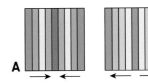

Measure and check the size of the square—if the measurement across the patchwork seams is less than 18½in, trim the top and bottom to square it up to size.

4. Rotary cut each square across both diagonals to make four (4) large triangles from each. *Fig. B*

Take care not to stretch the bias edges. Take the two (2) triangles from each set which have the strips running parallel to the long edge and rearrange them to form the centre square. *Fig. C*

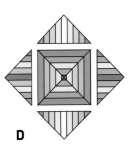

The triangles should alternate between warm and cool. Pin and sew the triangles together in pairs, nestling the seam allowances up against one another for precise piecing, to make two (2) larger tri-angles. Press seams towards the warm strips. Pin and sew these two large triangles together lining up the seams. Press seam allowance to one side. The centre square will measure 17¾in (or slightly less—see Technical Tip, previous page). Trim off any dog-ears as you go.

5. Take the remaining triangles with the strips running perpendicular to the long edge and sew these to the sides of the centre square. *Fig. D*

Sew the warm triangles first, on opposite sides of the square, as shown. Press seams towards the outer triangles. Sew the cool triangles to the remaining sides and press as before. The centre diamond panel will now measure 24⅞in square (check this measurement—see Step 6).

> ### Technical Tip
> Every time you sew a triangle to the side of a square (in this case the centre of the quilt), you will have a tiny triangle sticking out from the edge of the sewn seam, where it has been offset. Trim off these dog-ears as you go.

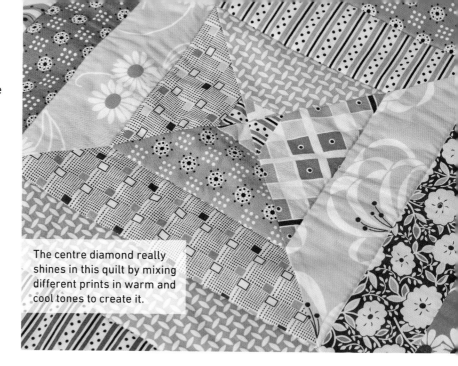

6. Take the two (2) 24⅞in × 2½in frame strips and sew to opposite sides of the centre diamond (if the centre diamond is smaller, cut these first two strips the same length as the diamond edge and add 4in to that measurement for the second pair). Press seams out towards the frame strips. Sew the two (2) 28⅞in frame strips to the remaining sides of the centre diamond. The centre diamond will measure 28⅞in square.

The centre diamond really shines in this quilt by mixing different prints in warm and cool tones to create it.

Making the Outer Triangles

7. Sort the thirty-four (34) 15¼in long strips into two (2) sets of seventeen (17) strips. Aim for similar numbers of warm and cool (or light and dark). Lay these out in order, shading from warm to cool and back again. Once again, sew them together in pairs, then sew pairs together to make two (2) rectangles, 15¼in × 34½in. From each rectangle, cut a right-angled triangle. To do this, centre the top point of the triangle in the middle of the ninth strip, and trim off the two corners with a 45-degree cut, then trim the base (as shown by the dashed lines) to 29⅝in wide (or the width across the central patchwork plus ¾in, if your patchwork centre has worked out slightly smaller). *Fig. E*

Set aside the four (4) trimmed-off corners. *Fig. F*

8. Sew together two (2) of the trimmed off corners to make one larger triangle. From this cut another right-angled triangle as in Step 7, making sure the top point of the triangle lines up with the middle of a strip. *Fig. G*

Repeat to make another triangle in the same way—you should now have a total of four (4) outer triangles.

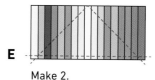

E   Make 2.

F   29⅝"

G   Make 2.

9. Pin and sew the first two (2) outer triangles to diagonally opposite edges of the centre diamond. Note that the outer triangles will form ⅜in dog-ears when the long edge is lined up with the edge of the centre diamond. Press seams in towards the frame. Repeat this step with the remaining two outer triangles. The centre will now measure 40½in (check this measurement—see Step 10). *Fig. H*

H

10. Take the two (2) 40½in frame strips and sew them to opposite edges of the centre (if the centre is smaller, cut these first two strips the same length as the edge of the panel instead of 40½in and add 4in to that measurement for the second pair). Press seam allowance towards the frame strips. Attach the two (2) 44½in frame strips to the final two edges. Again, press seam allowance out towards the frame strips.

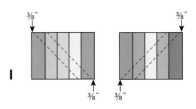

I

Making the Border

11. Take the eighty-eight (88) 7in × 2½in strips and sort into four (4) sets of twenty-two (22) pieces for each of the four outer borders. Arrange the strips to shade from warm to cool (or light to dark) in each. Sew together and press seams in one direction. Check that the borders are the same length as the quilt length and width.

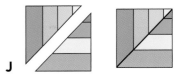

J

12. Sort the twenty (20) 7in strips for the faux mitre corners together into four (4) blocks of five (5) strips, two warm and two cool. These should continue the shading effect. Sew together and press the seam allowances in the same direction. From each rectangle, cut two (2) 45-degree triangles, starting the cut ⅜in from each end to allow for seam allowances. Cut the warm triangles on a 45-degree angle sloping up to the left and the cool triangles to the right (or the light and dark sloping in opposite directions, if you have a light/dark variation), as shown by the dashed lines. *Fig. I*

13. Pair one warm and one cool triangle, so the seamlines match up to create a faux mitre effect, pin and sew together. The seam allowances on two of the faux mitres squares will be lying in opposite directions—the other two will need to have one set of seam allowances pressed in the opposite direction to enable the seams to sit together neatly. Press the seams of two (2) faux mitre squares towards the warm colours and the other two (2) towards the cool colours. *Fig. J*

14. Place the mitre squares temporarily at the quilt corners to make sure the strips on the ends of the outer borders don't match adjacent mitre strips. Sew to either ends of two of the borders. Pressing the seams towards the mitre squares.

Technical Tip

If your quilt has come out slightly small and the pieced borders are therefore slightly too long, adjust the length by sewing a second seam slightly outside the first one on every other strip, starting from each end, until the border is the right length.

15. Lay out the quilt centre and arrange the borders around it to check that the faux mitre corners will be at the correct end of the shorter borders e.g. cool to cool, dark to dark etc. Attach the two shorter borders to the top and bottom of the quilt, first matching the two centre points and pinning together and then easing the edges to fit. Press seams towards the outer frame strips. *Fig. K*

The use of a bold, single print fabric for the frames really highlights and unifies the mix-and-match fabrics used in the patchwork.

16. Pin the two longer borders to the sides of the quilt in the same way. Sew and press as in Step 15. The quilt will now measure 57½in square.

17. Take the two (2) 57½in and two (2) 61½in outer framing strips (if the quilt is smaller, cut the first two strips the same length as the quilt and add 4in to that measurement for the second pair). Sew and press the framing strips to the quilt the same way as the frames in Steps 6 and 10.

Finishing Off

18. Quilt as desired. Simple quilting suits this patchwork though it would also suit a computerised longarm pattern or other all over design.

19. Join the binding strips with mitred seams, pressing the seams open. Press the binding strip in half along the length, and bind to finish, using either butted or mitred corners. Remember to add a label to help people identify your work in the future.

Layout diagram

Something Different

This design can be adapted to use strips of different widths. Susan's initial experiment with the pattern was made using 1½in strips instead of a Jelly Roll. The number and width of strips in the centre dictate the length of the strips—twenty-one (21) strips, 21½in long in this instance. The base measurement of the outer triangles is obtained by measuring the finished centre section and adding ¾in to allow for the dog-ear overlap at the ends, and the length of these strips can be half the centre section measurement plus an inch. The corner mitre sections will have ten (10) strips rather than five (5), and the border strips can be the same length as the Jelly Roll version. The fabrics used were all Japanese-style prints.

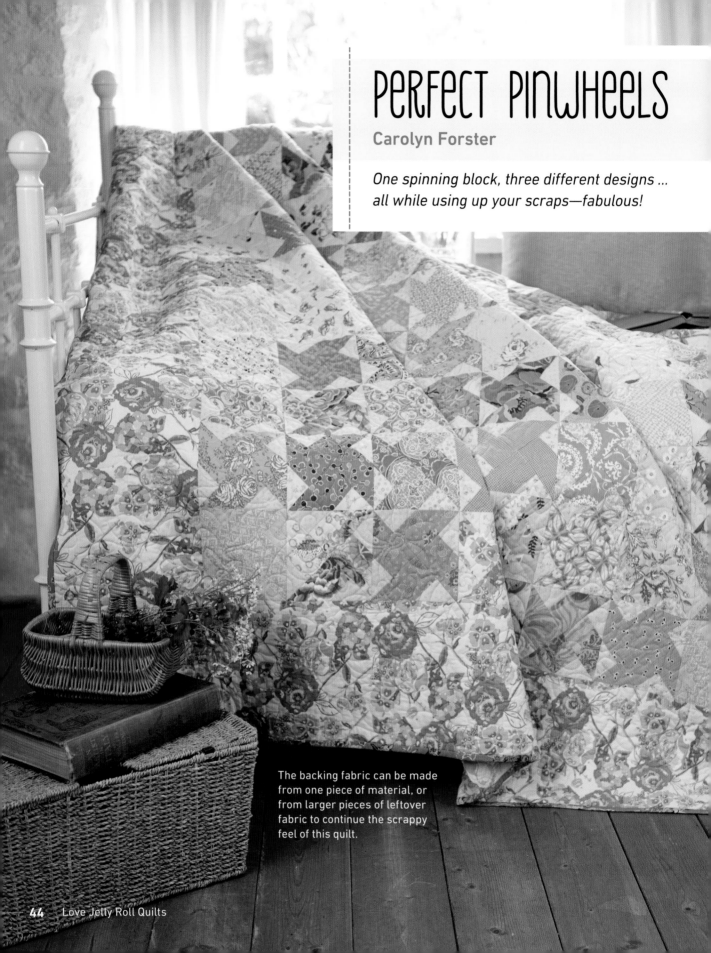

PERFECT PINWHEELS

Carolyn Forster

One spinning block, three different designs ... all while using up your scraps—fabulous!

The backing fabric can be made from one piece of material, or from larger pieces of leftover fabric to continue the scrappy feel of this quilt.

QUILT

Finished quilt:
73in square

Technical Tip

Choose border fabrics after the patchwork is finished. Once all your scrappy blocks are made and sewn together, you may find that the fabric you had in mind previously no longer works. Audition different fabrics alongside the patchwork to find the best match.

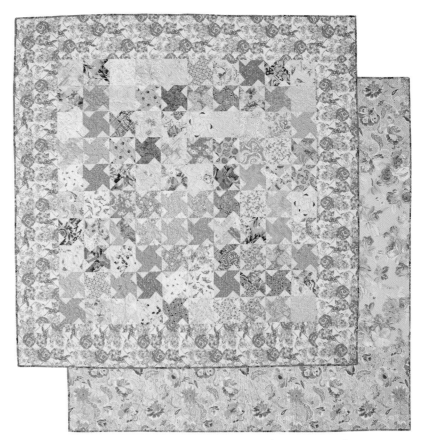

Quilted by Chris Farrance for the Quilt Room (quiltroom.co.uk)

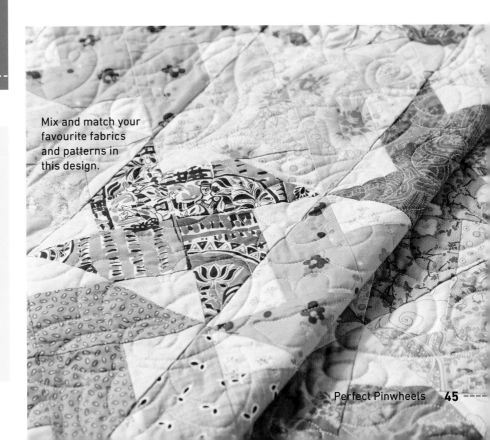

Mix and match your favourite fabrics and patterns in this design.

Behind The Quilt

Scraps Quilt

This is a great scrap quilt. You can use up all those leftover Jelly Roll strips and combine them into one of three different quilts, using the same technique and fabrics, but giving very different looks.

This quilt used all of the blocks from the cutting method that featured the green and turquoise prints as the pinwheels. The second quilt uses all of the remaining blocks with the light fabric featured as the pinwheels. And last but not least you could combine the two blocks to give a tessellating pinwheel quilt. This third quilt top is made from two fabrics only, and gives you an idea of the look created if you want to use up yardage rather than odd strips. If you want to take this quilt a stage further, then change the width of the strips, they can go fatter or thinner, just align the Half Square Triangle ruler accordingly. The yield from your sewn together strips will vary, as will the size of your quilt and blocks needed.

Cutting Out

1. From the light fabrics cut a total of fifty (50) 2½in × WOF strips.

2. From the dark fabrics cut a total of fifty (50) 2½in × WOF strips.

3. From the border fabric cut seven (7) 9½in wide strips. Remove the selvedges and join to one continuous length. Press seams open. Subcut as follows:

• Two (2) 55½in lengths.

• Two (2) 73½in lengths.

4. Cut the backing fabric into two (2) equal pieces. Remove the selvedges and join together along the long edge. Press seams open.

5. From the binding fabric cut eight (8) 2½in strips. Join to a continuous length with a bias join. Press seams open. Press along entire length wrong sides together.

Making the Blocks

6. Stitch one (1) light and one (1) dark strip together along the long edge, right sides together. Press seams towards the dark fabric. Make fifty (50).

7. Line up the template or 4in marking on your Half Square Triangle ruler with your strips. Make the first cut.

8. Rotate the template or ruler 180 degrees and make the second cut.

Repeat along the strip to cut a total of sixteen (16) triangles from each pieced strip.

9. Half of the triangles will have the light fabric in the wider section (lights) and half will have the dark fabric in the wider section (darks). Separate these lights and darks into two piles so as not to get muddled. Set the light triangles aside for the second quilt (see *Light Pinwheels*, page 52). *Fig. A*

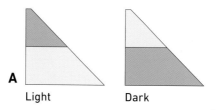

A Light   Dark

10. To make the blocks, take four (4) dark triangles, and sew them together in pairs, right sides together. Press seams open. *Fig. B*

11. Sew the pairs together matching the centre seam. Press seams open. Make one-hundred (100) 6in square blocks. *Fig. C*

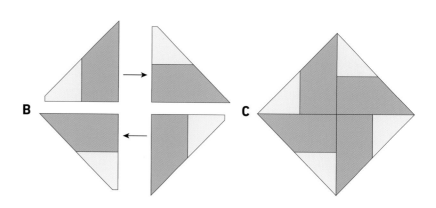

12. Lay out the blocks in a pleasing arrangement of ten (10) rows of ten (10) blocks.

13. Sew the blocks together to make a row. Press the seams in alternate directions in each row.

14. Sew the rows together. Press seams in one direction. *Fig. D*

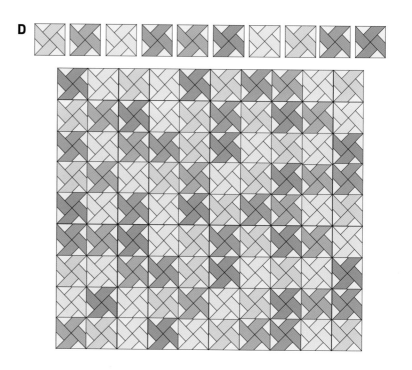

15. Stitch the short borders on opposite sides of the quilt. Press towards the border. Sew the remaining longer borders onto the top and bottom of the quilt. Press seams towards the border.

16. Layer and baste the quilt with backing and batting.

Layout diagram

Quilting and Finishing

17. Carolyn had the quilt longarm quilted in a swirly design, but if you wanted to quilt by hand, Amish Waves would work well for this.

18. To make Amish Waves with no template, start in the bottom right-hand corner of the quilt (left-hand corner if you are left handed). Place your thumb in the corner, your joint in line with the edge of the quilt. Use chalk or a Hera marker to draw around the top of your thumb, making the first curve. *Fig. E*

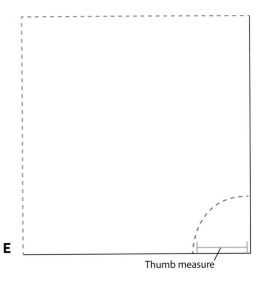

E

Thumb measure

Quilt this, then use the height of your thumb to the joint as the guide for the depth of the next curve measuring from the first curve. *Fig. F*

Mark the quilt, and progress on until the first set of curves or waves is as large as you like. *Fig. G*

19. To begin the second wave, sit your thumb next to the last line of quilting and mark as you did before. *Fig. H*

You will know now that you will be quilting the same amount of lines as the first wave to make the design. Don't worry if the arcs are slightly different in height, overall they will look consistent. You could also use the length of your quilting needle as a depth marker, but if your needle is larger, say for Big Stitch quilting, then the gaps will be deeper.

20. Continue in rows along the quilt until fully quilted. *Figs. I & J*

21. When it is quilted, remove any basting and bind and label the quilt to finish.

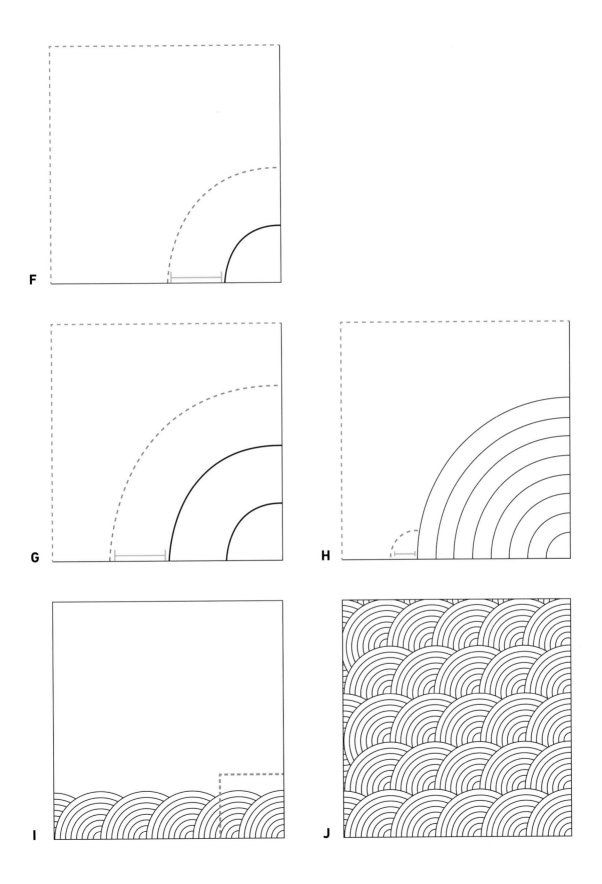

LIGHT PINWHEELS

Get even more from your scraps and make two quilts from one technique! Using the "light" blocks left over from the first quilt to make the pinwheels creates a completely different looking design ... and much of the work is already done! These would look excellent laid on twin beds or draped over facing sofas to create a coordinated look, but with their own individual style.

QUILT

Finished quilt:
50in square

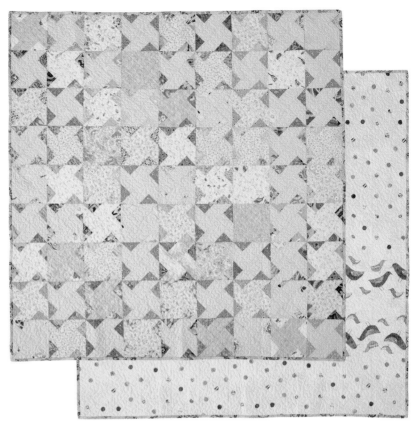

Create a different look by using the "light" half-square triangles instead of the "dark" ones.

Cutting Out

1. Cut the backing fabric into two equal pieces. Remove the selvedge and join together along the long edge. Press seams open.

2. From the binding fabric cut six (6) 2½in × WOF strips. Join to a continuous length with a bias join. Press seams open. Press along entire length wrong sides together.

Making the Quilt

3. To make the blocks, take four (4) light triangles, and sew them together in pairs, right sides together. Press seams open. *Fig. A*

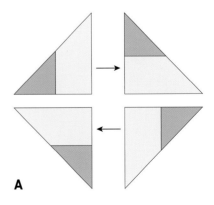

A

4. Sew the two pairs together matching the centre seam. Press seams open. Make eighty-one (81) blocks. You will have some leftover triangles which could be used in another quilt or matching pillows. *Fig. B*

5. Arrange the blocks into nine (9) rows of nine (9) blocks. Stitch the rows together and press the seams to one side, alternating the direction on each row.

6. Sew the rows together, press the seams in one direction.

7. Layer and baste ready to quilt. This quilt is quilted in an allover vermicelli design on the machine. This could be done at home as it is a simple pattern to reproduce on the sewing machine with free motion quilting.

8. Remove any basting, trim, bind and label.

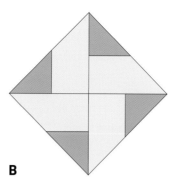

B

Layout diagram

The low-volume floral prints on the light fabric add delicate detail to the design.

Perfect Pinwheels 3

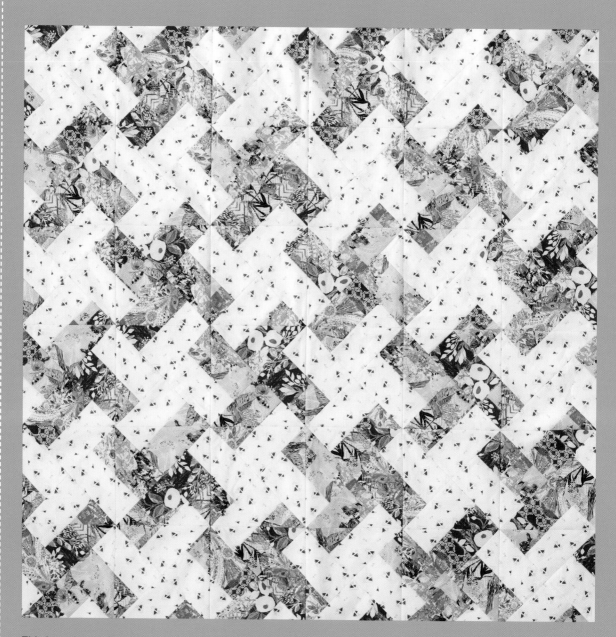

Third version of the quilt made using just two fabrics and both the light and dark blocks in alternate positions. This extends the pinwheel shapes into neighbouring blocks creating a tessellated effect. Use all the blocks to create a much larger quilt.

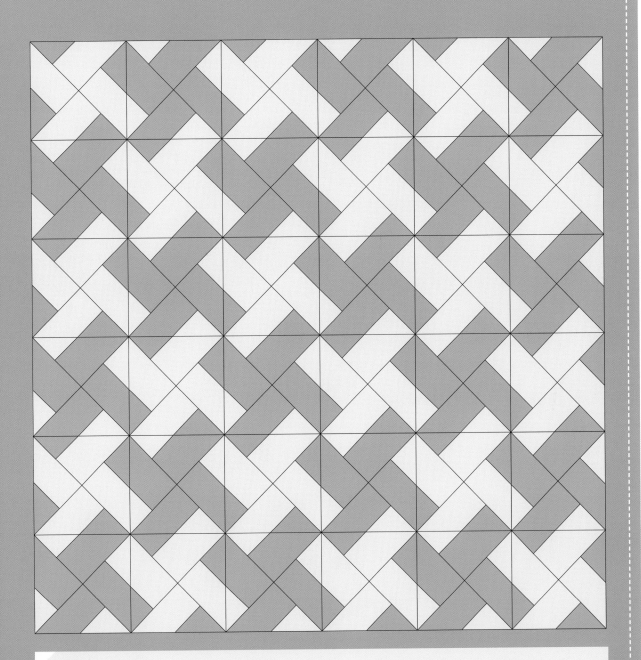

Technical Tip

To give this design yet another makeover, you could add borders and sashing to alter the size of the finished quilt. Try sashing between groups of nine blocks to space them apart and make the quilt larger.

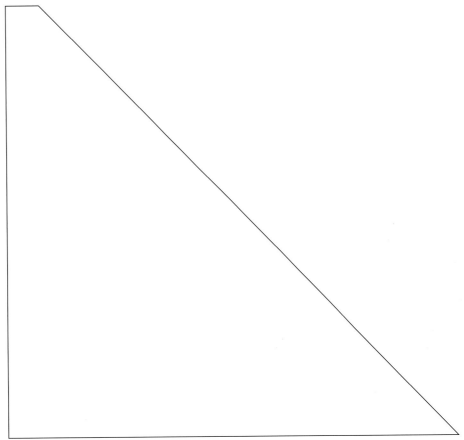

Template A

WOVEN RAINBOW QUILT

Carolyn Forster

Weave together your scraps of fabric to create a unique quilt that has its roots in designs from yesteryear.

Use scraps of colourful fabric to create this rainbow of strips that is sure to put a smile on anyone's face.

QUILT

Finished quilt:
52½in × 62½in

You Will Need

Background fabric: 1½yds

Weave fabrics: Forty (40) 2½in × 18in strips and eighteen (18) 2½in × 6½in strips, or one (1) Jelly Roll*

Batting: 63in × 73in

Backing fabric: 3½yds

Binding fabric: ½yd

If using a Jelly Roll, first cut into the forty (40) 2½in × 18in strips and eighteen (18) 2½in × 6½in strips before following "Cutting Out" list.

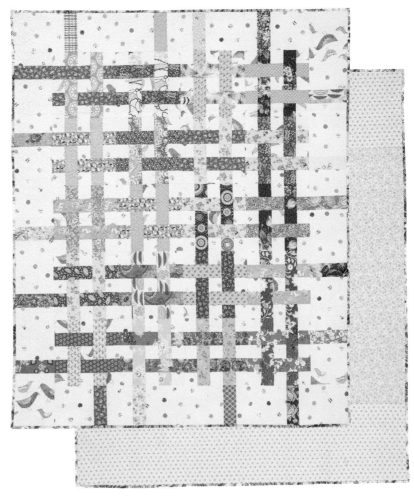

Quilted by The Quilt Room, Dorking

Cutting Out

1. From the background fabric cut, as follows:

- Twenty (20) 2½in squares (for the blocks).

- Eighty (80) 2½in × 5in strips (for the blocks).

- Two (2) 2½in × 6½in (for the border).

- Three (3) 4½in × 6½in (for the border).

- Two (2) 6½in × 6½in (for the border).

- Ten (10) 8½in × 6½in (for the border).

- Five (5) 12½in × 6½in (for the border).

2. From each of the assorted 2½in × 18in weave fabric strips cut as follows:

- Two (2) 2½in × 6½in strips.

- One (1) 2½in × 5in strip.

3. Cut the backing fabric into two equal lengths, remove selvedge and join along the length. Press seam open.

4. From the binding fabric cut seven (7) strips 2½in wide.

Behind the Quilt

Woven Rainbow Quilt

"Woven style blocks have long been popular with quiltmakers with published examples being seen in quilts from the 1930s through to modern versions in the 1980s in books by Valerie Campbell-Harding and Muriel Higgins. My block is a variation of one seen in a book by Chuck Nohara (*2001 New Blocks for Patchwork*, Quiltmania). I've spaced the fabrics slightly differently in my version to make the maths easier.

"The quilt below uses 20 blocks and has a 6in finished border with inserts of 2½in strips to extend the woven effect at random intervals. You can space the strips in the border as you like, but I have given the measurements for the way I did mine. I did not always use the same fabric that was in the block to extend into the border, but did choose a similar coloured fabric.

"You can be as controlled or as random as you like in your choice of fabrics to 'weave'. Try using just two colours to weave, or light blue and dark blue for example. This version is scrappy to use up odd ends, but you can use fabrics from precut Jelly Rolls. I have used one fabric in this quilt as the background and the border, but you can vary this fabric as long as they blend together as a background and do not fight against the woven fabrics. The block requires you to stitch partial seams in its construction method, and this is a great skill to learn as it opens up a whole new selection of blocks for you to be able to piece on the machine. I find these blocks quite addictive, and it is hard to stop at just stitching one quilt with them."

—*Carolyn Forster*

Use different patterned and colour fabrics to add interest.

Making the Blocks

5. Work on one block at a time choosing two different fabrics to weave in each block, fabric A and fabric B. Stitch a 2½in × 5in strip of background fabric to either side of a 2½in × 5in strip of each weave fabric to make two pieced strips. Press seams towards the weave fabric. *Fig. A*

6. Cross cut each of these units in half to make two of each colour. *Fig. B*

7. Take a 2½in × 6½in strip of fabric A and one of fabric B. Stitch the A strip to the B unit from Step 6, and the B strip to the A unit. *Fig. C*

Repeat with the other two units. Press the seams towards the long strip.

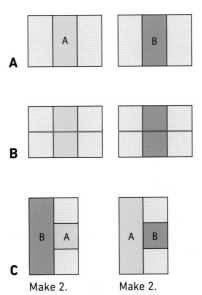

Make 2.   Make 2.

8. Now lay out the block as shown, centering the pieces around a 2½in square of background fabric. It is important that each block you make after this is laid out in the same way so that the quilt will create the woven effect. *Fig. D*

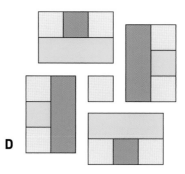

9. Start by sewing the middle background square to one of the surrounding pieces. Start at one end and stop stitching halfway along the seam. This seam will be completed at the end. Finger-press the pieced unit away from the centre square. *Fig. E*

D

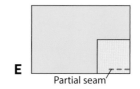

E

Partial seam

10. Now take the second pieced unit and attach it to the block, this time stitching all the way along the whole seam. Press this unit away from the centre square. *Fig. F*

F

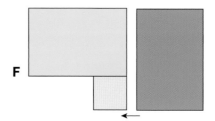

Continue adding the rest of the pieces until you just have the first partial seam to complete. *Fig. G*

Line up the raw edges and stitch from the outside in towards the seam you started at the beginning, backstitch to secure. Press towards the pieced unit. *Fig. H*

G

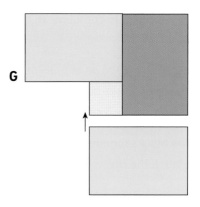

H

Completed seam

11. Repeat Steps 5–10 to complete all twenty (20) blocks. *Fig. I*

Lay them out in five (5) rows of four (4) blocks, rearranging until you are happy with the placement of fabrics. *Fig. J*

12. Stitch the blocks together, pressing the seams open, then stitch the rows together, pressing in the same way.

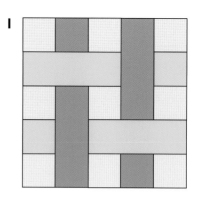

I

J

Making the Borders

13. Each of the borders is made slightly differently with the remaining 6½in wide background and weave fabric pieces. Make the top and bottom borders first following the diagram from Step 11 (previous page). It will help to lay the pieces around the quilt centre to get the placement right. The way the weave fabrics extend into the border is random, so feel free to rearrange the pieces to make the borders as you wish, but place similar colour fabrics together. Stitch the pieces together into one length and press the seams towards the background fabric. Add the borders to the top and bottom of the quilt top.

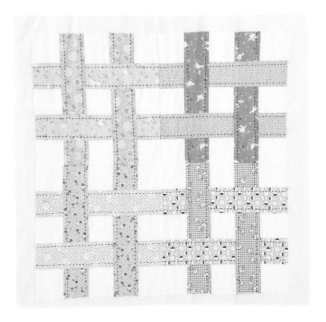

The sample on the top right shows how hand quilting with Big Stitch can really enhance these blocks. The two single blocks above show how the different placement of A and B units can reverse the "under/over" effect of the weave.

14. Make the side borders referring to the layout diagram or in your own arrangement. Press seams towards the background fabric. Add these borders to the sides to complete the quilt top.

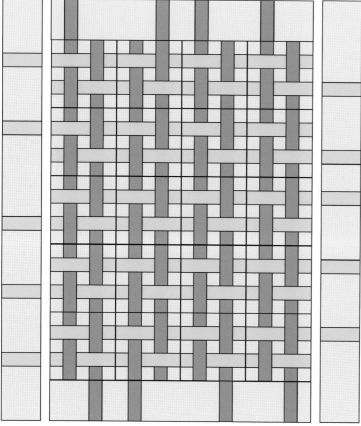

Layout diagram

Quilting and Finishing

15. Layer the quilt with backing and wadding and prepare to quilt.

16. Carolyn had her quilt quilted with an all over meander design. She also made a small sample to show an idea for hand quilting with Big Stitch and Perle cotton or cotton a broder thread (see the photos in Making the Borders, page 67). In this sample she outline quilted ¼in from the seams to emphasis the weave effect of the quilt.

17. When quilted, bind to complete and add a label.

BASKETS IN BLOOM

Nicola Dodd

Let pretty florals and fresh Flower Basket blocks flourish in your home with this contemporary twist on a classic design.

Brighten your home with vibrant greens and pretty floral tones this winter.

QUILT

Finished quilt:
62in × 67½in

Fabrics used: Flower Mill by Corey Yoder for Moda Fabrics + Supplies

You Will Need

One (1) Jelly Roll *or* twenty-seven (27) 2½in × WOF strips

Background fabric: 2¾yds

Border fabric: ¾yd

Batting: 70in × 76in

Backing fabric: 4¼yds

Binding fabric: ½yd

Quilted by Jayne Brereton at Quilter's Trading Post

Notes

• WOF = width of fabric

• Please read through the pattern before you begin, assuming a ¼in seam allowance and a fabric width of 42in.

Cutting Out

1. Choose nine (9) Jelly Roll (2½in × WOF) strips for the pots. From each strip, cut four (4) 2½in × 7½in pieces, which is enough for two (2) blocks.

2. Choose eighteen (18) Jelly Roll strips for the flowers. From each strip, cut as follows:

• Two (2) 2½in × 6in pieces.

• One (1) 2½in × 4½in piece.

• Four (4) 2½in squares.

• Two (2) 2½in × 2in pieces.

• From the trimmings, cut two (2) 2in squares.

Behind The Quilt

Pretty Posies

"I've always loved bringing flowers into the house, whether it's a bowl of garden roses, pots of forced bulbs or a flower-filled quilt. This block combines two traditional favourites, the Flower Basket and the Nosegay, but is pieced in an innovative way that avoids the inset seams and on-point setting of the originals. I chose Flower Mill by Corey Yoder for Moda as it included printed wovens, suggesting a basket weave, and brightly coloured prints on a rich charcoal grey, which reminded me of toleware."

—*Nicola Dodd*

3. From the background fabric, cut one (1) 7in × WOF strip. Subcut into four (4) 7in × 10in pieces (end fillers).

4. From the background fabric, cut thirty-four (34) 2½in × WOF strips, setting eleven (11) aside for the horizontal sashing and inner borders. Subcut the rest as follows:

- Thirteen (13) 2½in × 10in pieces (vertical sashing).

- Seventy-two (72) 2½in × 4½in pieces.

- Thirty-six (36) 2½in × 4in pieces.

- Seventy-two (72) 2½in squares.

- Thirty-six (36) 2½in × 2in pieces.

5. From the border fabric, cut six (6) 4½in × WOF strips.

6. From the binding fabric, cut seven (7) 2½in × WOF strips.

Piecing the Pots

7. Mark a 45-degree diagonal line at one (1) end of a 2½in × 4½in background piece. *Fig. A*

Place at a right angle at the other end of a 2½in × 7½in Jelly Roll (print) rectangle, right sides together. Sew along the marked line. *Fig. B*

Flip open and press before trimming away the back layers, ¼in away from the seam. *Fig. C*

A

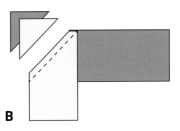

B

C

8. Repeat at the other end of the print piece with another 2½in × 4½in background piece. Draw the line in the opposite direction. Make two (2) using matching prints. *Fig. D*

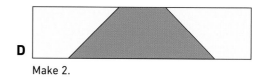

D
Make 2.

9. Join the two (2) matching units together, taking care to match the points. Press the seam open. Your unit should measure 4½in × 11½in. Make eighteen (18). *Fig. E*

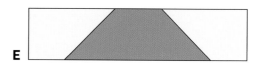

E

Piecing the Flowers

These will be pieced in three (3) rows. Choose three (3) fabrics for each flower unit. For each flower, you need:

- From print A, one (1) 2½in × 4½in piece and two (2) 2in squares.

- From print B, one (1) 2½in × 6in piece, two (2) 2½in squares and one (1) 2in × 2½in piece.

- From print C, one (1) 2½in × 6in piece, two (2) 2½in squares and one (1) 2in × 2½in piece.

- From the background, two (2) 2½in × 4in pieces, four (4) 2½in squares and two (2) 2in × 2½in pieces.

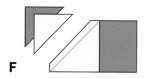

F

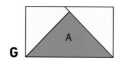

G

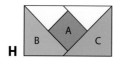

H

10. To make the top row, mark a diagonal line on the back of two (2) 2½in background squares and pin one (1), right sides together, to the end of a 2½in × 4½in print A piece. Stitch on the line, flip open and press (to snowball the corner). Trim away the back pieces. *Fig. F*

Join the remaining square to the other end in the same way, as shown. *Fig. G*

11. Repeat Step 10 to add two (2) different contrast print squares, B and C, to the bottom corners as shown. *Fig. H*

12. Join a 2½in × 4in background piece to each side, pressing away from the flower.

13. To make the middle row, join the short sides of two (2) 2in × 2½in print B and C pieces. Use the top row as a guide for fabric placement and press as directed. *Fig. I*

14. Join a matching 2in print A square to each side, followed by a 2in × 2½in background piece to each end, again pressing as directed.

15. To make the bottom row, snowball the lower left-hand corner of a 2½in × 6in print C piece with a 2½in background square. Snowball the upper right-hand corner with a 2½in print B square. *Fig. J*

16. Repeat Step 15 with a 2½in × 6in print B piece, a 2½in background square and a 2½in print C square. Take care to reverse the placement, as shown in Step 15 (above). Join the two (2) units together, pressing as directed.

17. Join the three (3) rows together to form the flower, pressing towards the centre row. Your unit should measure 6in × 11½in. Make eighteen (18) flowers. *Fig. K*

Assembling the Blocks

18. Choose a Pot unit and a Flower unit and join together, pressing the seam away from the Flower. Your unit should measure 10in × 11½in. Make eighteen (18).

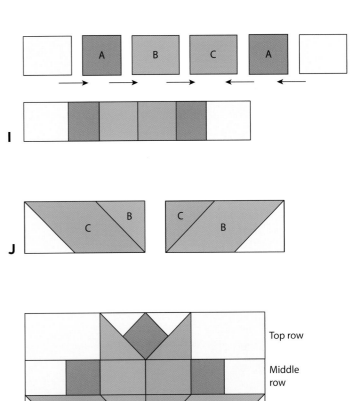

I

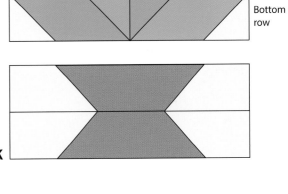

J

Top row

Middle row

Bottom row

K

Assembling the Quilt

19. Assemble the quilt centre, as shown in the layout diagram, joining the blocks, vertical sashing and end filler pieces together to form rows. Join the rows and horizontal sashing together to form the quilt centre, pressing seams towards the sashing as you go.

20. Add the inner and outer borders to the quilt, measuring each side of the quilt centre first and joining strips to make longer lengths where needed. Press away from the quilt centre.

Layout diagram

Quilting and Finishing

21. Cut your backing into two (2) equal pieces, trim off the selvedges and join together along the long edge using a ½in seam. Press open, then trim to 70in × 76in.

22. Sandwich the batting between the backing and the quilt top, baste, then machine or hand quilt.

23. Join your binding strips and press in half, wrong sides together, along its length. Trim away excess batting and background—taking the opportunity to ensure your corners are square—and bind the raw edge using your preferred method.

CANDY CRUSH

Natalie Santini

For a pixel-perfect finish, try this Mexican sugar-skull inspired quilt.

LIFE IS SWEET
Reclaim the Day of the Dead for the living with this colourful throw—the free-motion quilting adds a whimsical feel that suits the sweet shades.

QUILT

Finished quilt:
56in × 66in approx

You Will Need

One (1) Jelly Roll, assorted pastel colours (We used Kona New Pastels.)

Background fabric (white): 2¾yds

Backing fabric: 60in × 70in

Batting: 60in × 70in

Binding fabric: ½yd

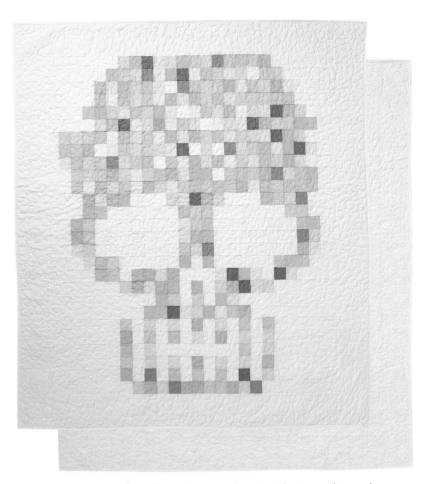

We love how the quilt creates a cool contrast between the candy colours and the cream background.

Note

Change the mood of the quilt by changing the colour of the background fabric to black, or try using vibrant neon shades instead of pastels.

Notes

- Seam allowances are ¼in throughout.
- Press seams open, unless otherwise instructed.
- A Jelly Roll is a set of 2½in × 42in strips. You will need at least twenty-two strips.
- WOF = width of fabric

Cutting Out

1. From the Jelly Roll strips, trim sixty-six (66) 2½in × 10in strips in a random assortment of colours. Cut eighty (80) 2½in squares from the remaining strips.

2. From the background fabric, cut:

- Two (2) 6½in × 44½in border strips
- Two (2) 6½in × 66½in border strips
- Twelve (12) 2½in × WOF strips
- Ninety-seven (97) 2½in squares

3. From the binding fabric cut seven (7) 2½in × WOF strips.

Strip piecing makes sewing all those squares a doddle!

Preparing the Pieces

4. Working with the pastel 2½in × 10in strips, take three strips (use a random selection of colours) and sew together along the long edges, to make a strip set that measures 10in × 6½in. Cut this into four (4) 2½in × 6½in pieces to make four three-square strips. These pieces are Unit A.

Repeat to sew and cut twenty-two (22) sets of three strips, to give you a total of eighty-five (85) Unit A pieces.

5. Repeat the process in Step 4, but this time using three 2½in × WOF background strips and sew these together. You will need to sew four of these strip sets to cut a total of fifty-two (52) 2½in × 6½in pieces. These pieces are Unit B.

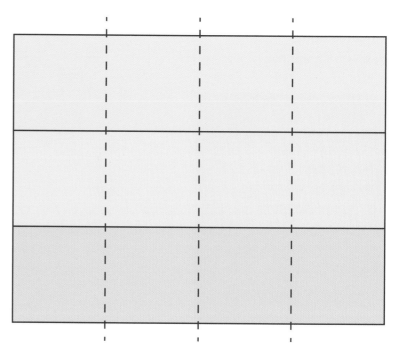

Combine a variety of sweet shades to create the Unit A pieces.

Piecing the Quilt Top

6. Following the layout diagram, lay out your pieces row by row. To help you arrange the pieces, the diagram is shaded as follows: Unit A shaded pink, 2½in pastel squares shaded blue, and the Unit B and 2½in background squares shaded white.

7. If you don't have space to lay out all your pieces at once, work one row at a time, marking off the rows on a copy of the diagram as you complete them.

8. Sew all the pieces in the first row together, pressing the seams open. Then move onto the next row and so on until all the rows are sewn together.

9. Once you've pieced each row, you can sew the rows together, carefully matching up the seams. Press the seams open or to one side, as preferred.

10. Sew the 6½in × 44½in border strips to the top and bottom of your quilt top, then sew the 6½in × 66½in border strips to either side of the quilt.

Try using contrasting quilt
patterns on the skull and
the background.

11. Make a quilt sandwich and baste using your preferred method. Quilt as desired—we used an allover free-motion stipple design. Trim away any excess batting and backing, and square up your quilt.

12. Sew your binding strips together along the short edges into one long length. Press in half, wrong sides together and use to bind your quilt.

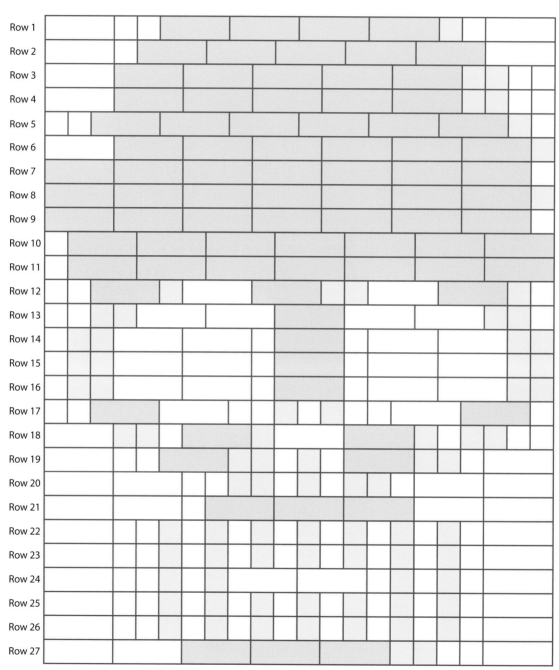

Layout diagram

BRILLIANT BIRDS & BUDS

Carolyn Forster

Use up your scraps with this fun appliqué project that can also be worked on while out and about!

Bring nature indoors with this delightful design that feels like you're wrapped in a glorious summer's day!

QUILT

Finished quilt:
70½in square

You Will Need

Background fabric:
1¼yds × WOF

Block border fabric: Twenty-four (24) 2½in × WOF strips (60in total), *or* one-hundred-and-ninety-two (192) 2½in × 4½in scraps

Scraps for flowers:
10in × WOF *or* sixty-four (64) 2½in squares

Scraps for leaves:
20in × WOF *or* one-hundred-and-twenty-eight (128) 2½in squares

Cotton Perle size 8 or 12 *or* **stranded cotton embroidery thread***

Three different fabrics for border: ½yd of each

Binding fabric: 20in × WOF

Backing fabric: 4½yds

Batting: 80in square

Appliqué templates (page 93)

Template plastic (*optional*)

Freezer paper if using

* If you choose a variegated co-loured thread, then you get a nice variety of shading on the stems.

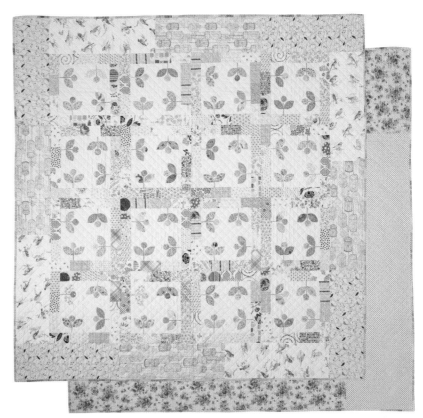

Machine quilted by Chris Farrance for the Quilt Room (quiltroom.co.uk)

Notes

- To supplement yardage you're working with, use charm squares, mini charms or Jelly Rolls. Their sizes work really well with the dimensions required for lots of the pieces in this quilt, plus give you lots more fabric choices.

- You could even use a charm pack or Jelly Roll as the starting point for the colour choices in your quilt.

- If using the stranded cotton you may wish to split it to three strands for working, or whatever your desired thickness.

Gorgeous fabrics can really shine in this quilt, so choose your favourites and show them off!

Behind The Quilt

Brilliant Birds & Buds

This project was inspired by a small quilt I made for the book *Little Quilts and Gifts from Jelly Roll Scraps* (published by Search Press). As is often the case, when I make little projects, they inspire something larger. I loved the block and all of the ideas it suggested, from the different arrangements of the flowers within the block to the possibilities even of doing this as a quilt-as-you-go project. This was a great quilt to use up many scraps. The simple appliqué was fun to do, and worked on the blocks before they go together, so they made a nice portable take along project. The partial pieced border frames around the blocks meant that I could position them in any orientation in the quilt, and is a great technique to add to your repertoire.

Cutting Out

1. From the background fabric cut as follows:

• Sixteen (16) 10½in squares.

2. From the block border fabrics cut as follows:

• One-hundred-and-ninety-two (192) 2½in × 4½in pieces.

3. From the flowers fabric cut as follows:

• Sixty-four (64) circles using template A (page 93).

4. From the leaves fabric cut as follows:

• One-hundred-and-twenty-eight (128) leaves using template B (page 93).

5. From the border fabric cut as follows:

• Four (4) 7½in × 21½in strips from each of the three fabrics.

6. From the binding fabric cut as follows:

• Eight (8) 2½in × WOF strips and join to a continuous length with bias joins. Press along the length wrong sides together.

7. Cut the backing fabric into two equal lengths. Remove the selvedge, and join together along the long edge. Press seam open.

Making the Blocks

8. To make one block, take one (1) white background square and twelve (12) block border strips. Stitch the strips together along the short edges into four (4) rows of three (3). You can press the seams open.

9. Frame the square using a partial piecing method. With right sides together, align the first strip with one side of the square. Stitch along the seam stopping about 2in from the end of the square leaving the end loose. Finish off the thread and remove from the machine. Finger-press the seam towards the frame. *Fig. A*

10. Take the second frame unit and align with the background square and first frame edge. This frame will cover the entire side. Stitch the whole seam and then press seams towards the frame. *Fig. B*

Continue on until all frames are sewn and pressed. *Fig. C*

Partial seam

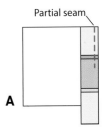

A

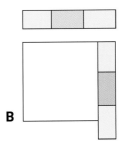

B

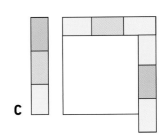

C

11. Now go back to the first frame, which is still loose at one end. Finish off the seam overlapping the original line of stitching to secure. Press with the iron. Make sixteen (16) framed blocks in this way. *Fig. D*

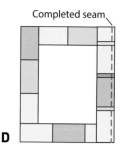

Completed seam

D

> ### Technical Tip
>
> Windmill style borders using the partial seam technique can look especially effective when using stripes, chevrons or other directional prints. Try adding multiple frames with prints going in opposite directions for a dynamic effect.

Making the Appliqué

12. Prepare the flower circles. Use the template (page 93) to cut the circles or you can easily cut these by folding the square into quarters and cutting a curve. Open out and you will have a circle.

13. Thread a needle with sewing thread and tie a knot in the end. Start with a backstitch then sew a small running stitch ⅛in away from the raw edge all around.

14. When you get to the beginning, gently pull the thread to gather up the edges of the circle. *Fig. E*

E

Stitch a few stitches in place to secure the thread on the back, then flatten out the circle. Making small circles this way gives them a little bit of filling to bulk them out slightly, and saves turning under fiddly edges. Make four (4) for each block.

15. Prepare the leaves. You can use whichever method you favour, but I used freezer paper for my appliqué here.

> ### Technical Tip
>
> You are often able to re-use the freezer paper a number of times until its stick is lost, so you don't need to cut a freezer paper template for every individual piece of appliqué, saving you time.

16. Take the freezer paper and fold it into layers with the dull side on top. Transfer a leaf shape (page 93) onto the top layer by drawing around it. Use a stapler to then hold the layers together, and cut out along the drawn line. Now remove the staple to release the layers. This way you don't have to draw around the shapes so many times.

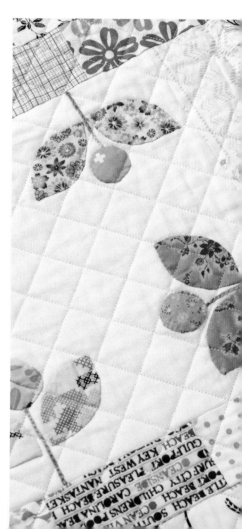

17. Position the freezer paper shapes on the back of the fabric, leaving enough space around them for a scant ¼in seam allowance. *Fig. F*

Place them shiny side down and use a hot iron to "glue" the shapes to the fabric. Cut each shape out adding the scant ¼in seam allowance around all edges. *Fig. G*

18. With a needle and tacking thread, make a knot in the end and start stitching from the front of the shape, turning the seam allowance over to the back. Secure with a backstitch and continue around the shape in this way turning the edges under. *Fig. H*

You may need to clip some of the curves to turn the seam allowance over smoothly. Repeat to make all the appliqué pieces. *Fig. I*

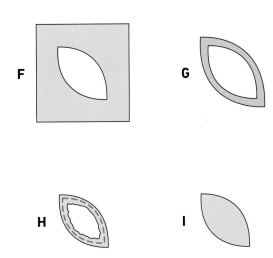

F G

H I

Freezer paper is a useful tool for making appliqué shapes. Leave the paper in while you hand stitch the shapes down. It can then be removed at the end by making a small slit through the background fabric on the back of the quilt and slipping the piece of paper out. It is not necessary to sew the slit closed.

19. Place the appliqué pieces so that the leaves are 1in from the base and ¾in from the side of the block. *Fig. J*

Leave a tiny gap between the leaves to have room to embroider the stem. You could play around with the positions of the flowers; see Appliqué Layout Ideas (below) for some ideas. Appliqué the pieces in place.

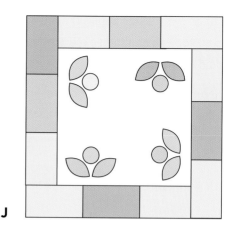

J

Appliqué Layout Ideas

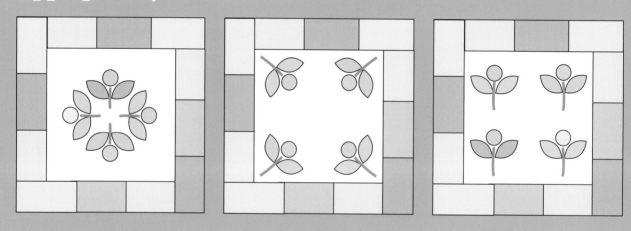

20. Now embroider the stem from the base to the flower head. *Fig. K*

I used chain stitch and a variegated thread. You could also choose a whipstitch or split stitch depending on your preference. This is a good project if you want to use up odd ends of embroidery threads, I like the variation of the stems being slightly different colours which is why I like to use variegated thread.

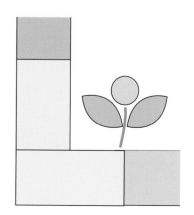

K

21. Chain stitch can be used effectively as an outline and it adds more texture than the backstitch. Start with a knot and bring the needle up to the right side of the fabric. Hold the thread in a loop while the needle is returned to the point where you started. Insert the needle into the fabric and come up a short distance away, drawing the thread up through the loop. Do not pull tight. Repeat to create a row of chain stitches. On the back you will have a row of backstitches.

22. When all sixteen (16) blocks are finished arrange them in a pleasing layout of four (4) rows of four (4) blocks. There are no seams to worry about matching or colliding due to the windmill style frames.

23. Stitch the blocks together in rows, pressing the seams in alternating directions. Sew the rows together. Press all the seams in one direction.

24. Now sew the strips for the outer border together. There are four (4) strips from each of the three fabrics. Each border has three strips, one of each fabric. Stitch together and press seams open.

25. Stitch the border strips to the quilt using the same partial-seam technique in Steps 9–11.

26. Layer and baste with backing and batting and quilt as desired. The sample is quilted with a crosshatch design. You can machine quilt yours like this by marking out guide lines with a Hera Marker or masking tape, and a long ruler.

27. To hand quilt I would outline quilt the appliqué first, and then quilt the crosshatch around the appliqué. Big stitch quilting would make this process faster.

28. Once quilted remove any basting and bind the quilt and label.

Technical Tip

Appliqué can be cut from random parts of the fabric or you can choose to fussy cut details from the pattern to frame a motif such as a flower head, leaf or animal. Making a transparent plastic template can help to centre the shape, especially if you wish to cut the same motif multiple times from the same print.

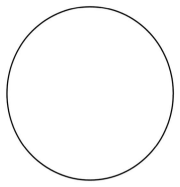

Template A

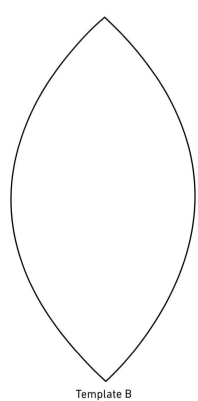

Template B

ABOUT THE CONTRIBUTORS

Check out these contributor websites for more great content! For additional resources, visit *Love Patchwork & Quilting* at lovepatchworkandquilting.com and *Today's Quilter* at todaysquilter.com.

Jo Avery
(Scotland)

Granny Squares (page 12) originally appeared in issue 23 of *Love Patchwork & Quilting* (Immediate Media).

Website: mybearpaw.com

Instagram: @mybearpaw

Susan Briscoe
(United Kingdom)

Dryslwyn Dreams (page 18) and *Super Strips Medallion Quilt* (page 34) originally appeared in issues 1 and 6 of *Today's Quilter* (Immediate Media).

Website: susanbriscoe.com

Nicola Dodd
(United Kingdom)

Baskets in Bloom (page 70) originally appeared in issue 43 of *Today's Quilter* (Immediate Media).

Website: cakestandquilts.com

Instagram: @nicolajdodd

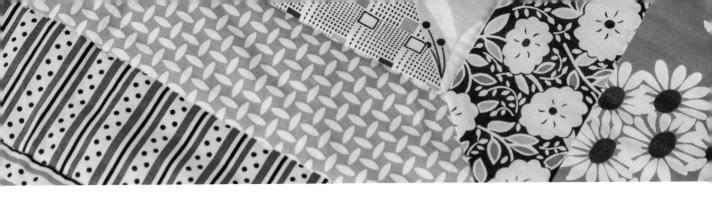

Carolyn Forster
(United Kingdom)

Perfect Pinwheels (page 44) and *Light Pinwheels* (page 52), *Woven Rainbow Quilt* (page 60), and *Brilliant Birds & Buds* (page 84) originally appeared in issues 11, 17, and 9 of *Today's Quilter* (Immediate Media).

Website: carolynforster.co.uk

Instagram: @quiltingonthego

Alice Hadley
(United Kingdom)

Cuddle Up (page 28) originally appeared in issue 16 of *Love Patchwork & Quilting* (Immediate Media).

Website: lovepatchworkandquilting.com

Instagram: @lovequiltingmag

Natalie Santini
(United States)

Good Karma (page 6) and *Candy Crush* (page 78) originally appeared in issues 36 and 26 of *Love Patchwork & Quilting* (Immediate Media).

Website: www.hungryhippiesews.com

Instagram: @sewhungryhippie

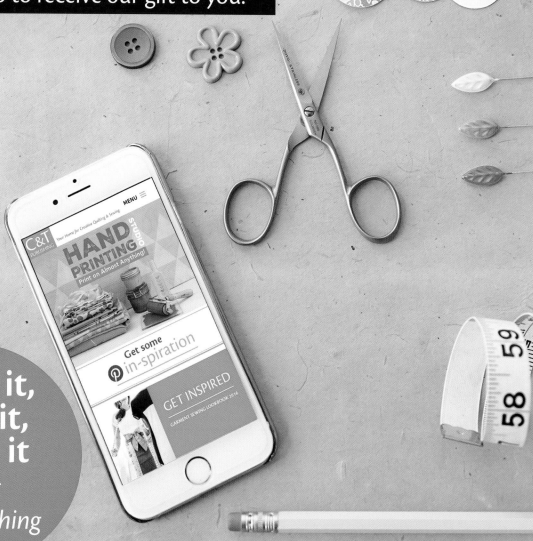